THE NETWORKING MENTOR

MENTOR

Whose Story are You In?

(2nd Edition of I Love Networking)

W0008514

DEDICATION

We'd like to thank our editors, Karen Rought for her work on the first edition of this book (*I Love Networking*) and to Heidi Scott Giusto who contributed immensely to the second edition of this book (retitled to *The Networking Mentor*). We'd also like to thank Dorian Prin for her amazing cover and Colin Horner for his fun visual graphics relating to the many ideas we shared in this book. *We would recommend each and every one of them to you without hesitation.*

We would like to thank the mentors in our lives who helped guide us to be a better version of ourselves. We'd also like to thank the mentees in our lives for helping us to remember the fundamentals of success and to learn how to communicate those fundamentals to others.

TABLE OF CONTENTS

PROLOGUE

From our experience in the networking group BNI, we have learned that mentors can make a huge difference in people's success at networking. We've written this book based on these experiences in BNI; however, *we believe that these experiences translate into many different types of networking organizations.*

Each and every one of us has people in our lives who made a difference. We all have someone in our story who influenced the path we took—or perhaps motivated us to carve our own path. These are the mentors we've had in our life. Their impact can be life changing.

We firmly believe in the power of mentors to make a positive difference in the lives of others. By devoting time and attention to a mentoring relationship, both parties reap deeply powerful and meaningful rewards that extend well beyond simple financial gain.

As we mature and gain more experience, we have the opportunity to transition from mostly being a mentee to also being a mentor. *This book is for both mentors and mentees.* Because we believe in lifelong learning, we feel we can always be a mentee in some area of our life. However, we also believe that as we gain more experience, we have an obligation to contribute to others and to help them learn from our experiences (both good and bad). The act of mentoring also propels the mentor to further growth and knowledge. Teachers often say they learn from their students, and our experience has taught us that the mentoring relationship benefits both parties. This experience can't be understated. We have both learned that *we learn* when *we teach* others.

We've all had mentors who are in "our story." When we talk about how our life has changed through our experiences with them, they are part of that story. However, there is something even more important: **The real question is not who's in our story but whose story are we in? Whose life have we made a difference in?** That's what creates a meaningful life, and that's why this book is for both mentees and mentors.

—Ivan Misner, Ph.D. & C. G. Cooper

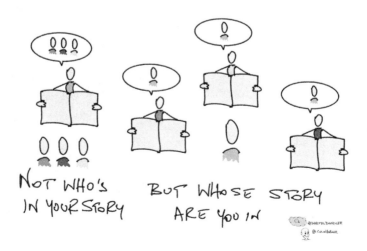

CHAPTER 1

STRUGGLING

I sat waiting for my client to arrive. Let me clarify. This was my biggest client...by far. In fact, if it wasn't for his repeat business, I might not have made payroll for my three employees on more than one occasion.

Dusting off the small conference room table with a napkin, I didn't even notice Jim walk through the door.

"You don't have to do that for me, Ken."

I must've jumped in surprise because Jim struggled to stifle a laugh.

"I, uh, it was my turn to clean up the office," I offered lamely. "Have a seat. Can I get you anything?"

"Some water would be great, thanks."

Hurrying to fetch two bottles of water, I passed my bemused office manager, Dana. She'd obviously let Jim in the door without warning me. I wondered silently if she'd have done that if she knew how tight we were on cash. I still ran the finances, and I hoped Dana had no clue. I'd already dipped into my personal savings to pay her. How much longer could I keep up the juggling act? I tried to force the thought away as I returned to the conference room and handed Jim his water.

"How are things going?" I asked, eager to see how we could do more business together.

"Pretty fantastic. I hope we haven't overwhelmed you with the uptick in orders."

I shook my head emphatically. "No problem. We can handle anything you throw at us," I said, even as I wondered whether we could, in fact, deliver. "What can I help you with? You said it couldn't wait."

Jim nodded and pulled two envelopes out of his coat pocket. He slid them across the table. "One of those is our updated order. I thought I'd bring it by."

I opened the envelope as casually as I could, but my eyes widened at the numbers. The new order was fully twice the size of any previous order. "Looks like business is good."

Jim smiled. "We've been very fortunate. Thanks for helping us along the way."

I nodded and felt my legs shake under the table. It was exciting to get such a large order, but doubt crept in. Could our small company deliver in time? I picked up the second envelope.

"That one is an invitation. I'm part of a local networking group. We're looking to give more business to a company just like yours. We're interviewing people in your profession to find someone who we could give all of our referrals to. I think you might make a great candidate. I was hoping you'd stop by so I could introduce you to some of my best local contacts."

The thought of more business sounded good. Coming from Jim made it even better. Almost every referral he'd ever given me turned into a sale. I sometimes wondered how he did it.

It was the mention of networking that made me queasy. I'd tried business networking in the past. There were the wasted fees and time spent at networking meetings. Then there was the one and only after-hours young professionals cocktail session I'd attended. I think I talked to one person and spent the rest of the time checking my phone.

Networking was not something I did well. I wasn't a schmoozer. It was about as far out of my comfort zone as singing in front of a stadium full of people.

"Gee, thanks, Jim, but I'm…"

"I know what you're thinking. It wasn't my thing either. What would you say if I told you that over seventy percent of our company revenue came from that one networking group?"

My mouth dropped open, and I snapped my jaw shut as quickly as I could. "You're kidding."

Jim shook his head. "Just a few short years ago I was on the verge of bankruptcy. Now, well, you see how much I'm using your services. So what do you say? Worst case, I'm buying you breakfast and you get to meet more business owners."

I nodded as thoughts spun and nerves frizzle-frazzled. He waited patiently for my response. Jim's company had been a loyal customer for over a year. He'd even stayed with us when we'd delivered an order two days late. I knew him as a straight shooter, someone who wouldn't put a friend in harm's way. Even so, my suspicious nature and fear made me gulp. My mouth felt sandpaper dry and a trickle of sweat slipped down my spine.

Against the screaming fear in my gut, I croaked, "Okay. I'll be there."

PRACTICE

For Mentees

Many people *say* they get most of their business from referrals. Liar, liar, pants on fire! The vast majority of people cannot state how they actually get those referrals…which usually means they, in fact, are *not* getting most business from referrals. Rather, that claim reflects a common desire among many business owners much more than reality. So, how can business owners actually go about getting most of their business from referrals? They need a plan and a way to execute it if they want to accomplish that goal.

If you're new to networking, Jim's reaction might feel very familiar to you. What resonated with you in this chapter? What obstacles do you have to overcome before you can network effectively? What action steps can you take today to conquer these hurdles, to create a plan and then execute that plan?

For Mentors

As you go about your day-to-day business, observe others around you. Who seems to be struggling? Who seems to *always* be hustling…so much so that it looks like they haven't slept in a week? Take note and offer a valuable suggestion that someone in the past offered you. Consider offering to take them to lunch, so you can learn more about their needs and how you can help. You might be surprised at how good you feel after doing this good deed. Plus, you will almost always improve your skills when you help others improve their skills. It is truly a win-win situation.

CHAPTER 2

THE MEETING

I almost didn't have time to worry about the networking meeting with the work that Jim's order had created. Our little team worked overtime to get it done early. One thing my father, a convenience store owner for thirty-five years, had always told me was to "under promise and over deliver." It had become sort of a mantra I repeated often to my employees.

When Wednesday morning came, I rose early and took a shower. My wife, Heidi, had already left for the hospital. She was a nurse, and a darn good one.

I mentally ran through my daily routine as I lathered and rinsed. A glob of soap plopped into my eye, and it reminded me of the dreaded meeting starting in less than an hour. *Who schedules a networking meeting so early in the morning?* I thought as the shampoo sting subsided and I shut off the water.

Rushing to put on my work clothes, a pair of pressed khakis and a collared shirt, I decided to skip my morning coffee. My nerves were already in a twist and adding caffeine to the mix would only give me a sour stomach. I grabbed a banana and a stack of business cards as I hurried out the door, wondering what the morning would hold.

+++

Twenty minutes later, I arrived at the upscale restaurant listed on Jim's invitation. There were already a few cars in the parking lot. I looked around to see if people were getting out of their cars. Nope. All clear.

Taking a deep breath, I stepped into the dew-misted morning. The only sounds were the birds and my thudding heart. I willed myself to relax, but the feeling only got worse as I reached the door. Making an entrance was not one of my gifts. I always imagined walking in with my zipper down, shaving cream on my neck or a coffee stain on my shirt. You might say I was a bit of a worrier.

I checked myself in the mirrored glass and opened the door.

Inside were small signs pointing the way. I followed them and the sounds of laughter. This was it, my last chance to turn back.

Before I could think to go back, a voice called out, "Good morning! You must be Ken."

I looked to my right and realized I'd almost walked by a small welcome table where a middle-aged woman stood with a big smile.

"Uh, yeah. I'm here…"

"I know. You're Jim's guest. Welcome!"

My face must have given away my surprise.

She laughed. "Sorry. We like to know who our visitors are so we can try to get you some business." She waved her

9

hands in the air dramatically. "My apologies. I'm Sharon."

I shook her hand as I tried to square my shoulders and wipe the look of dread from my face.

"Here's your name tag. I'm going take you right through there." She pointed to the next room where all the commotion was coming from. "I think you're really going to like it."

I gulped as she led the way.

The room was filled with what looked like forty people. I was surprised to see the joviality so early in the morning. Jim spotted me as soon as we walked in.

"Hey, Ken! Glad you could make it."

"Thanks for having me," I responded, as convincingly as I could.

"I want to introduce you to some people."

Jim proceeded to take me from group to group and present me to his friends. I was surprised to see three of my customers, but then realized I'd met them through Jim. I started to relax as they did all the work. Everyone asked me about my business, and I answered as best I could. Before I knew it, a bell rang. Jim quickly ushered me to grab a plate of food, and then we took our seats.

I looked around the room as I ate and the meeting commenced. The President of the group introduced her leadership team and some others. I was surprised to learn there was an Education Coordinator and that "lifelong learning" was a core value of the group. Education and networking had never been paired before at other events I had attended. Jim saw the surprise on my face and leaned over as if he was going to tell me a secret.

"Do you remember those courses you took in college about networking? About how it's crucial for business success?"

I looked at him puzzled.

"Me neither. Because **we don't teach networking in colleges and universities anywhere in the world.** I learned everything I know about networking through this group. It fills the education gap." These words from Jim, indeed, made me feel like I learned a powerful secret.

WE DON'T TEACH NETWORKING
IN UNIVERSITIES & COLLEGES

I continued to process Jim's remarks as I noticed how excited everyone seemed. Maybe there was something in the coffee.

The introduction segued into an educational spot about networking and then what they called the members' weekly presentation. I froze. The President, a very professional and well-known accountant with a snappy sense of humor, said visitors would give their presentations after the members. I put my fork down slowly. I'd lost my appetite.

11

n't worry about it," whispered Jim. "Just tell everyone who you are, what you do and what kind of client you're looking for."

I nodded mutely and silently cursed myself for being so naïve. I was trapped. Public speaking was another one of my weaknesses.

Unable to listen to many of the members giving their brief talks because of the throbbing in my head, I hastily scribbled a few notes on a piece of paper I found on the table. Name. Company. Client.

I tried to focus on what people were saying. They seemed to have a similar way of delivering their message. I filed it away in preparation for my doomed speech.

"Okay," said the President. "Now that we've heard from our members, if I can have our visitors stand up when I call your name. Please tell us who you are, the company you represent, what you do and what kind of customer you're looking for."

I was the third to be called. On the bright side, one of the guys that went before me was so nervous that he knocked down not one, but two glasses of water on his table. Rising when called, I tried to smile as I stuttered through my hastily prepared speech. I have no idea what I said.

I sat down heavily, relief flooding through my body. *Made it.*

"Good job," whispered Jim. "I think you might have some referrals coming your way. I told you, our group needs your company."

The thought brightened my mood almost as fast as the relief of being out of the limelight. I sat back and listened to

12

the final parts of the meeting, glad to be through my ordeal. The Vice President stood up and gave the statistics for the group. I didn't understand most of what he said until he talked about the closed business that had been passed between members. My ears perked up. I was all about the bottom line. This was it. This was my out. If the numbers stunk, I would politely ask Jim not to invite me again.

"So far this year our group has passed…"

I listened in shock and peered around the room. How could a group of that size generate so much business? It had to be a trick, something to snag new members. But none of the members flinched. In fact, a look of pride settled over their faces. It was like a football team that knew they were good, but didn't flaunt it unless they were on the field. Something pulled at my chest. I wanted what they felt.

The President wrapped up the meeting with, "Visitors, thank you for coming today. We'd love to have you consider applying to be part of our group. If you meet with the Visitor Host, who is in the corner at the back, you can get a quick orientation of how the organization runs. There, you'll learn about our meetings, educational programs and requirements."

As I started to gather my things and get out of my chair after meeting with the Visitor Host, two members, whom I recognized as Mike and Jesse, stepped up to talk to me.

"Hey, Ken, we were wondering if you could give us a quick rundown of what your company does," said Mike. "Jim speaks very highly of you and suggested we talk to you about a project Jesse and I are working on. We want something very specific. We've tried two other companies, but no one seems to understand what we need."

"What is it I can help you with?" I asked. This was familiar territory for me. I knew my business inside and out. Nerves were gone. I was back. All business.

They explained the dilemma. I asked a few questions to make sure I understood their need. I knew we could help them.

"How about I get you a proposal this afternoon?" I asked.

"That would be excellent!" said Jesse.

We shook hands and exchanged business cards.

"So? What did you think?" Jim asked as we walked toward the exit.

"It's not what I expected."

"How so?" he asked, with a grin.

"Everyone was just so...nice. Nobody tried to sell me anything. Everyone wanted to know about me. Aside from having to give my commercial, it was pretty good. Heck, I might even get some business out of it."

Jim nodded knowingly. "See? And you were so against networking."

He was right. It wasn't anything like I'd experienced before. I was used to networking events where I was on my own, trying to get my business card into as many hands as I could. Most networking groups I'd gone to in the past were a hubbub of face-to-face cold calling. That morning's meeting was different. It was like a well-rehearsed play. Everyone knew their part. At no time did I feel alone or awkward. They'd made me feel welcome and wanted.

"Hey, I almost forgot. We got your order wrapped up last night," I announced.

Jim smiled and patted me on the shoulder. "I think you're

just what this group needs." We shook hands and I headed to my car.

Maybe I need to look into this networking thing, I thought as I pulled out of the parking lot.

PRACTICE

For Mentees

Networking doesn't have to be painful. In fact, if it is, then you're either doing it wrong or you're in the wrong place. If you're serious about growing your business, consider joining a local structured networking group like BNI. Unlike some networking groups, organizations like BNI take the guesswork out of networking. They have a proven system that walks you through how to be a master networker *and* how to grow your business. They're also smaller and less intimidating.

Your homework is to go online to look for a good networking group. For a BNI chapter near you, go to **http://ivan.bni.com** for help in locating a group.

Get out of your comfort zone and visit a couple groups. Find one that fits your personality. Ask members how the group has helped their business. You may be happily surprised by their answers!

For Mentors

If you're attending your weekly BNI meeting or other networking event, be mindful of people whose facial expressions and body language silently shout, "I don't know what I'm doing here or what I'm supposed to say!" Introduce yourself and ask them who they are and what their business is. Welcome them to the group and ask if they have questions. **Act like a host not a guest**. It's always a great way to network.

CHAPTER 3

THE DECISION

I churned out the proposal for Mike and Jesse in record time. Despite my lack of sleep over the past few days, I felt energized. Something about the networking meeting lit a spark in me. I guess I hadn't realized I'd lost it.

Mike called me the following morning and thanked me for the proposal. He had some questions that I answered without missing a beat. At the end of the conversation, he asked me to send over the contract and said that they'd have it back to me before the end of the day. I must've looked like a grinning fool as I set my phone down and leaned back in my chair.

With the order from Jim and the new contract with Mike and Jesse, I'd make payroll for at least two months. I might even be able to pay myself.

+++

The days flew by as I attacked my business with renewed vigor. I cleaned up processes, collected outstanding invoices and called on customers. As I dug into my company, I realized there were things I'd done to sabotage our efforts. It was little things like giving excessive discounts or not following up on proposals. Let's just say that with the weight of the world on my shoulders, my mind hadn't been as sharp as it should've been. I would do better.

In the meantime, I got two calls from other members of Jim's networking group. One I couldn't help, but the other turned into a small order. It wasn't minutes after getting the signed contract that Jim called.

"Hey, Ken! How's it going?"

"Pretty busy around here. Before I forget, I wanted to thank you again for inviting me to your group."

I told him about the deal I'd closed.

"That is fantastic! Anything else I can help you with?"

I hesitated. He was on my list of people to call, but I'd put it off with the excuse that I was too busy. I shook off my timidity and opened my mouth, "I was thinking about maybe…um…I was wondering what you thought about me putting in an application to join your group."

"That would be awesome. I knew from the moment I met you that you'd be a good fit. I already got a call from Mike and Jesse telling me how impressed they were with your proposal. I think they'll be a good customer and advocate."

"Yeah, so what do I need to do now?"

Jim explained the process as I took notes. The group met every week and there was an application and interview process. They wanted committed members. I'd have to draw a little extra from the company's funds for the membership fee, but if the past week were any indication, I'd make my money back in no time.

But I still hesitated.

"Jim, can I ask you one more question before I decide?"

"Sure. What's on your mind?"

"Well, that number keeps nagging at me…the number I heard announced at the meeting…the amount of closed business. Look, I'm not that outgoing. I don't meet with a million people every week. I'm not sure if I'll be able to make enough referrals."

"That is a great question for me to hear!"

"WHAT?!?" My head spun. That was not what I was expecting to hear. "Can you explain?"

"That question shows you are a *perfect* person to join our group. Because it shows you care. It shows you want to do your part. **We can't teach you to have desire to help others, but we can teach you how to give referrals.**"

I felt a wave of relief wash over me. I thanked Jim again and promised to see him the following Wednesday.

PRACTICE

For Mentees

It's time to make a decision. By now you understand the value of focused networking just like Ken. Remember, in order for networking to work, you have to put in the effort. Networking is not a magic pill that spawns new business overnight. Networking is a commitment. **Networking is more about farming than it is about hunting.** It's about developing long-term professional relationships.

NETWORKING IS MORE ABOUT FARMING THAN HUNTING

Review the groups you've visited. Write down the pros and cons of each and how you think they'll help your business grow. Think about whom you've met, how you can help them and how they could help you. Focus more on the giving than the receiving.

If you're ready, contact the group and tell them you're interested in joining. Welcome to the team!

For Mentors

If you know someone thinking of joining your networking group or your BNI group, offer to take them to lunch so they can ask you questions. Many people have questions that, as a member, you might have long-forgotten you had at one time. Don't be surprised if someone asks "Is this for me?" If they do, ask them "Do you want to build your business?"

Whether people are doing okay, struggling or doing well, the desire to grow transcends all three positions. **Networking**

groups like BNI accelerate the rate at which people walk through the door.

People also often wonder whether networking is best suited for people in particular industries. Reassure them that **to have success in a networking group like BNI, it's ten percent profession and ninety percent person.** Having a mindset focused on growth and helping others matter above everything else.

CHAPTER 4

THE COMMITTEE

Thankfully my nerves were only fifty percent as frazzled as they'd been the week before. It had been a productive Monday and Tuesday. We were on a roll. I was energized, and so was my little team. My wife remarked how positive I seemed and how excited I was to go into the office. Heidi even mentioned that I looked more confident and that I was carrying myself differently.

I was a happy man walking into the networking meeting on Wednesday morning. Once again, the ever-smiling Sharon greeted me at the door.

"I heard you put in an application, Ken. That's great!" She beamed.

"Yeah, I hope they take it easy on me during the interview."

Sharon waved her hand like she was shooing a fly on its way. I stuck on my nametag and stepped into the meeting space.

The session was conducted almost identically to the week before. They obviously had the system down. With my nerves somewhat at bay, and my presentation prepared, I was able to concentrate more on what people were saying.

There was a wide variety of professions assembled, and by the time the members were halfway through their commercials, I remembered what Jim had told me. The group rules only allowed one seat per professional classification. That meant that there could only be one plumber or one accountant in the group. I relaxed even more at the thought. It felt like I was about to be in the catbird seat.

I was the first of the six visitors to be called on to stand and give my infomercial. As steadily as I could, I read my prepared speech. I saw a couple members nodding and jotting notes as I sat down.

The meeting wrapped up precisely on time, and I waited patiently for the Membership Committee to call me in for my interview. I mingled with the people I knew and even stretched my skills by introducing myself to the Education Coordinator. All in all, I was feeling pretty good about myself.

A few minutes later, Jim poked his head in the door. "We're ready for you, Ken."

I followed him into a back room and took the seat at the head of the table when offered by the Vice President, who also headed the Membership Committee.

The Vice President, a bespectacled gentleman named Phillip who held the financial planning seat in the group, introduced the Membership Committee and told me that the references I'd given on my application had come back with flying colors.

"We also know you've done business with Jim for quite a while, and he has nothing but great things to say about you. All that being said, we want to make sure you're a good fit for our group. Many of us have been members for years and that makes us very proud and protective of our group. We don't let just anyone join."

"I can totally understand that," I said, as beads of sweat formed on my scalp.

"Good. Now, we could quiz you about your background and skill set, but what we really want to know is that you'll be committed to this group. Have you heard our philosophy?"

I had. They said it repeatedly throughout the meeting. "Giver's Gain®?"

"Do you understand what that means?"

"Give before you receive?" I answered.

"That's right," said Phillip. "Of course, we're all here to make more money, but we also believe wholeheartedly in the philosophy of Giver's Gain. If I help you, more than likely, you'll want to help me. Does that make sense?"

"Sure. It's how I've always run my business."

Jim raised his hand, and Phillip nodded for him to speak. "Let me explain why we bring up Giver's Gain. Nine times out of ten, members who end up leaving disgruntled are the ones who often don't take our philosophy to heart. I'm sure everyone around this table can tell you a time or two when they've temporarily forgotten to live by it. I'm guilty of it too. The trick is to keep reminding yourself to give first."

A woman named Kelly, the chiropractor of the group, chimed in. "I know what we're saying seems almost extreme, but it is an eye-opening experience for many people, me being one. When I first joined, it was all about me, me, me. I was so focused on my business that I didn't understand the key was to build relationships, not to book more clients. If I built relationships by helping others, the clients would come."

"That brings me to another point," said Phillip. "We want to make sure that you know getting business from the group is not a given. You still have to hold up your end of the deal."

"How do I do that?" I asked.

Phillip slid a single sheet of paper across the table. "This is our Code of Ethics. If and when you're inducted, you'll have to say this aloud along with the rest of our members." He tapped on the paper. "We take these words very seriously. Of course, if someone's professional association has a slightly different standard, like an attorney whose rules might be stricter, their standard supersedes ours."

I nodded and looked down at the Code of Ethics.

CODE OF ETHICS

1. *I will provide the quality of services at the price that I have quoted.*
2. *I will be truthful with the members and their referrals.*
3. *I will build goodwill and trust among the members and their referrals.*
4. *I will take responsibility for following up on the referrals I receive.*
5. *I will live up to the ethical standards of my profession.*
6. *I will display a positive and supportive attitude.*

(Professional standards outlined in a formal code of conduct for any profession supersede the above standards.)
© **1986-2019 BNI**

It sounded exactly like the way I did business.

"Make sense?" Phillip asked.

"Completely."

"Great. We take the Code of Ethics seriously. It helps us build a supportive culture where everyone benefits—from old members to new, from mentors to mentees."

I nodded my head in understanding.

"Unless anyone has any more questions..." He looked around the table. Everyone shook their heads. "...You'll be hearing from us in a couple days."

I stood up from the table and shook everyone's hands. Jim walked me to the door and left me with a final parting thought, "Good job today. Fingers crossed!"

He turned and walked back into the committee meeting. I left thinking that maybe I wasn't as much of a shoo-in as I'd thought.

PRACTICE

For Mentees and Mentors

By now, you've either joined a networking group or you're pretty close. The behavior under BNI's Code of Ethics that Ken was introduced to should apply to all of your networking activities—for both mentees and mentors. These are wonderful words to live and do business by. Take them with you on your journey. Refer to them often.

CHAPTER 5

THE NAYSAYER

I got a call the next day from Phillip. "Ken, it's official. We'd like to extend an invitation to join our group as a full member."

We chatted for a few minutes and he told me that I'd be inducted the following Wednesday. He also said that I'd learn about the *Member Success Program* after the meeting and that Jim had volunteered to be my mentor as I figured out how the group worked. I was excited to learn that this chapter assigned a mentor to each new member, which seemed like proof that they take the whole education thing seriously.

"Jim's a poster boy for failure and success in networking. He's the perfect person to show you how to maximize its effectiveness. I've gotta run, but I'll see you next week. Congratulations, Ken!"

"Thanks!"

I put my phone down and a smile crept its way across my face. It was an honor to be admitted into such a successful group, but the fact that Jim had volunteered to mentor me personally…well that really felt good. I wanted my business to be like his. Hopefully he would help me get there.

Dana walked into my office and said, "Your eleven o'clock is here."

"Is that Barry?"

She nodded with an amused look as I groaned. Barry was one of those customers you always walked on eggshells with. He could be good one month, behind on paying the next, nitpicky on a bad day. Sometimes I wished I had the courage to either set him straight or drop him as a client. Unfortunately, my business wasn't strong enough for that yet.

I took a calming breath and asked her to bring him in.

Barry walked in a minute later. "Hey, Ken! How's it going?"

I got out of my chair and shook his hand. "Pretty good. Can't complain."

"Well that's great. Let me tell you how my morning's been..."

Barry proceeded to tell me the latest in the saga of unbelievable stories of this client losing the contract leading to a delay, and on and on. He could talk a rock to sleep, I'm sure.

I listened and tried to pretend that I was really into what he was saying. It wasn't easy. There had to be a punch line coming. There always was with Barry. I braced for the request for a rush order minus our standard expedite fee, or maybe it was something else.

"So anyway, like I was saying, I'm gonna need this order as soon as you can get it," he finished.

I didn't want or need the headache, but instead of denying his request, I said, "Sure, Barry. We can make it happen."

"Great! I knew you would." He babbled on about how amazing we were, showering me with enough fluff that I could almost taste the feathers and cotton balls.

He stopped midsentence and pointed to my desk. "Hey, is that *The Oath*?" He said "The Oath" like it was some mysterious tome from the ancient Sumerians.

"It's called the Code of Ethics. I just joined this networking group——."

Barry didn't let me finish. "The one that meets on Wednesday? Jim, Phillip, Susan, and the rest?"

I perked up. "You know them?"

"Of course! I was a member of the group for a while. Things didn't work out."

He'd pricked my curiosity. "Can I ask why?"

Barry mulled the question over. He looked around as if to make sure no one was listening. I unconsciously moved closer.

"Let's just say the goods aren't exactly what's advertised," he said in a grim tone. "Have you been inducted yet?"

I shook my head, suddenly nervous.

"You may want to think twice. I'm not saying it's a bad group; you might just want to sleep on it. There were a lot of rules, and it took a lot of time. I'm too busy for that type of structure, you know what I mean?"

Nodding quietly, I steered the conversation back to his order. I was grateful he had the paperwork filled out for once. I thanked him for coming in and said I'd call when his shipment arrived.

I closed the door behind him and grabbed my sour stomach. I'd already paid my annual membership dues, and now I was hearing that it might've been a mistake. Did they dupe me? Would I have time for this commitment?

Rushing past a surprised office manager, I slammed my office door, picked up the phone and dialed Jim's number.

He picked up on the second ring.

"Hey, Ken! What's going on?"

I took a moment to calm my breathing. Jim must have sensed my unease.

"Everything okay?" he asked.

"I don't know…I just wanted to make sure joining your networking group was really a good idea."

"Well, I've already told you my story, and I know you've talked to some other members. Is there anything else I can answer for you?" His tone was soothing.

"I just…I don't want to make a mistake, you know?"

"I understand. Tell you what, why don't you tell me what happened? It sounds like something caused you to have doubts."

He waited patiently for me to answer. I tried to find the words.

"Was a guy named Barry part of your group?" I asked, willing myself not to say it through gritted teeth.

"Yeah. Is he a client of yours?"

"He is."

"Let me guess. He said some things about the group?"

"He did. He told me about all the rules and how much time this will take me. I can't afford to lose money by networking, Jim."

Jim actually chuckled. That threw me. "Sorry. Didn't mean to laugh. I've known Barry for a while. I used to do business with him."

"Used to?"

"Yes, he…tell you what. It's almost lunchtime. How about I buy you lunch and explain?"

I felt like a sucker, but I said, "Okay."

My fuming had calmed by the time I pulled my old car into the small strip center. Jim was waiting outside the sandwich shop.

"Let's grab a seat," he said and led the way inside.

He didn't speak until we'd ordered our food and sat down. I wasn't hungry.

"I can see you're still upset," Jim said.

I shrugged.

"You want me to tell you about Barry?"

I nodded.

"Good." Jim took a bite of his sandwich, chewed and swallowed before continuing. "Barry joined our group right around the same time I did. Nice guy. Liked to talk."

I grunted.

"Anyway, Barry did pretty well after joining. I think he got business from at least half the people in the group. He runs a service business that's in high demand, so giving him business was easy. After a couple months, we started hearing grumbles from a couple members. I happened to be filling in as Secretary/Treasurer while the sitting officer was on maternity leave. The President of the chapter had received two complaints about Barry's service. From what I can remember, he either wasn't delivering on time or he didn't perform to standard."

That sounded like the Barry I knew. "What did the group do?"

"The Vice President was tasked with tactfully talking to Barry about the complaints. Keep in mind that we want everyone to succeed. The *Member Success Program, Passport to Success Program, Mentor Program, BNI University* and other training programs are all there for a reason. These systems are in place to help new members, not hurt them. The Vice President met with Barry and told him. Barry was extremely apologetic. He promised there would be no more incidents and that he'd fix whatever needed fixing."

I was starting to see where the story was headed. My stomach finally settled, and I welcomed a bite of my Italian sub. All of a sudden I was starved. Jim smiled when he saw me eating.

"Things got better, but not for long. Soon Barry was absent more often than not. He wouldn't return calls. Basically, he broke every rule for success that we have. He didn't renew his membership with the excuse that he had too much business."

Jim went on to say, "Our organization has rules because they are necessary for success. **One of the strengths of a network is that most of the members are friends. One of the weaknesses of a network is that most of the members are friends.** Friends don't like to hold friends accountable. But in business, accountability is key. The systems, processes and rules help to keep us all accountable. **Hockey without rules would be boxing on ice!**" I laughed at that last truism.

HOCKEY WITHOUT RULES
WOULD BE BOXING ON ICE

@DIGITALDOODLER
@COLINHORNER

"Also," Jim continued, "if he talked to you about how much time networking takes, let me say this: Time is money. And money is time. Surely you are paying advertisers each and every month, right?"

I nodded my head in agreement. *Who doesn't pay for advertising?*

"The money you pay advertisers is important. . . and it represents your time. After all, you had to work to earn that money to pay advertisers. How would you feel if you could greatly reduce how much money you spend on advertising? Then would you have time to network?"

I felt like an idiot. I'd actually let Barry pull me in with his distortion of the facts.

"I'm sorry, Jim."

"For what?"

"I shouldn't have listened to him. I trust you, and today I doubted that trust."

Jim waved the apology away. "Don't worry about it. I'm just glad you called me. A lesser man would have let the worry fester until it turned into something much worse than indecision. I really think you're going to be an important part of our group, Ken. Don't let one naysayer ruin that."

I nodded solemnly and the conversation drifted to happier topics as we finished our meal.

PRACTICE

For Mentees

There will always be naysayers in your life. The question isn't whether they exist; it's whether you'll actually listen to them. **Sometimes people complain like it's an Olympic event (for the record, it's not). Don't give these people space in your head.**

As we've mentioned before, networking takes work. Not everyone will put forth the effort needed to succeed. **It's not "netsit" or "neteat." It's called "network!" While you should have a good time, don't make the mistake of confusing networking groups for social clubs. Both are fine and both are different.**

Here's your practice: Understand that there will be naysayers in your networking future. She may be a disgruntled member or a bitter former member. You'll hear things like, "That didn't work for me," "You shouldn't waste your money" or "That was a waste of time."

If you've done your due diligence, asked the right questions and gotten feedback from members, then you have nothing to worry about. **Whether you fail or succeed is up to you**. Say the following statement to yourself:

I will get out of networking what I put into it.

Say it every time you doubt your efforts. Say it every time you meet a naysayer. Say it every time you drag yourself out of bed in the morning wishing you could sleep for one more hour. Use it as your mantra to fend off distraction and doubt. Through iteration and frequent reminders, you'll learn to appreciate the value of building relationships through your networking efforts.

<u>For Mentors:</u>

Remember back to the day when you first thought about joining a networking group. Even if it seems like a foregone conclusion at this point, recall how big the decision felt at the time. Be patient in answering questions of people who might join. It takes time to create unconscious competence in a field. Your mentee needs your guidance in getting there. As their mentor, take time to appreciate the satisfaction you'll feel from knowing you're helping someone else grow their business like someone undoubtedly helped you.

CHAPTER 6

THE VCP PROCESS®

The next Wednesday, two of us were sworn into the group. Somehow I didn't screw up the Code of Ethics as I repeated the lines after the President said them. Raucous applause greeted us into the group, along with handshakes and back slaps.

I took my seat next to Jim and smiled inwardly. It felt right.

After the meeting, I stayed behind with Jim. He said that in many ways, he started our mentoring relationship related to networking the day he dropped by my office with the large order. He knew he wanted to help me grow my business but also shared that he would benefit from our relationship, too, which I found surprising until he explained that mentors tend to sharpen their skills and learn from their mentees. He realized this quirk of mentoring after coaching his daughter's chess team. **By coaching the kids, his game actually improved.** Now that I was officially a member of the group, Ken said it was time to move forward in earnest.

I was extremely eager to learn. I'd gotten another order a

day earlier from one of Jim's referrals and was feeling pretty good about my prospects. I was excited to learn I wouldn't have to figure out everything on my own and that Jim, along with numerous additional mentors, would help me get my footing.

"Today I wanted to talk to you about the VCP Process," Jim said, extracting a yellow pad from his briefcase.

"What's that?"

"VCP stands for Visibility, Credibility and Profitability. It's kind of a ladder you want to climb. Like the rungs of a ladder, you have to go one step at a time to get to the top. Another way to think about it is as a process. Through the process of building trusting relationships, you move along the VCP Process—or up the ladder."

I looked down at the yellow pad as Jim wrote Visibility, Credibility and Profitability from left to right across the top of the sheet. He then drew a long vertical line between each one to make three columns.

"When you first meet someone you want to do business with, how well do you know them?"

"Uh, not very well?"

"Right. So what you're saying is that you're a stranger to one another, correct?"

"Yes."

Jim circled the word Visibility. "We all start at the Visibility stage. As a business owner, you want people to know that you exist. Once they know your business exists, and can place you by name, you have gained Visibility with them. You with me so far?"

I nodded.

Jim moved his pen over and circled Credibility. "The next step, or phase in this process, is Credibility. What do you think that means?"

"I guess that means that someone thinks you're an honest person, credible, and they'd likely do business with you."

"Exactly. When you hit the Credibility phase with members of this group, it means they're now open to giving you business and referrals. They find you trustworthy and are willing to put their name on the line to send you business."

"So you're saying that until I have credibility, I won't get business?"

"Pretty much. Think about it. Would you do business with someone you didn't trust?"

"No."

"There are exceptions, of course, but for the most part people do business or buy products with a brand they recognize as being credible. The last phase of the process is Profitability, which means you've not only busted through the trust barrier, but you're also a go-to person for referrals. In Profitability, your worth to your referral partner is high. You are an important part of their world. This may not just relate to business and referrals. It often encompasses your personal lives as well. Make sense?"

I nodded as I watched him write names in each of the three columns.

"I've been a member of this group for three years. During that time, I've established some very strong working relationships. What I'm doing now," Jim nodded toward the paper, "is writing down where each member of our group ranks on my VCP Process. Remember, this group is my sales force. If I establish trusted rapport with them, they refer me to their friends, family and clients."

I'd never thought of the networking group being my sales force, but it made sense. They multiplied my ability to connect with potential customers. It was like having salespeople out in the field drumming up business.

I was surprised to see that most of the names Jim had written were under the Credibility column. There were a couple, including me, in the Visibility column, and a handful under Profitability. I asked him why that was.

"These members under Visibility are fairly new. I haven't yet had the time to develop the relationships."

Seeing my place in his Visibility column, I interrupted Jim's train of thought. "I feel bad that I'm in that column. After all the business you've brought me, surely I should be bringing you business…"

Jim waved the thought away. "You didn't know how. Now that you've brought this up, let me take a moment to teach you the technique related to the Language of Referrals—and how you can start giving, and getting, more referrals. I think you'll find that the more referrals you give, the more you'll get."

"We are all, each and every day, standing in the middle of referrals. They are all around us—we just aren't paying enough attention to them. Part of our brain has something called a 'reticular activating system.' Your reticular activating system is like a filter between your conscious and your subconscious mind. It is capable of taking instructions from your conscious mind and passing them on to your subconscious mind. For example, have you ever been in a busy airport with announcements coming over the loudspeaker, noise from all the hustle and bustle, people talking all around you but then your name or your flight number is announced and all of a sudden you stop what you're doing because you realize they said something that you needed to hear?"

I nodded my head, wondering where Jim was going with this.

"That's your reticular activating system at work. Your subconscious screens out things that you determine aren't important, and it alerts you about things you think are important. We have that same power as it relates to referrals. As I already said, **"we are all standing in the middle of referrals every day. They are all around us."** We simply need to put our reticular activating system to work in order to hear them. For that to happen, we need to start by listening for the Language of Referrals. Whenever anyone says to you, "I can't, I need, I want or I don't know," whatever they say next is most likely a referral for someone! These phrases (along with many others) indicate that the person talking is in need of something. That something they need is a possible referral that you can give. If you train your reticular activating system to open its filter and recognize those phrases you will almost immediately increase the amount of referrals that you can give to your referral partners."

Motivated by this powerful lesson, I made a mental note to be on the lookout for business for Jim.

Jim turned his attention back to explaining the VCP Process. "Now, the people I listed under Credibility know me, and some are my best friends. That doesn't mean they've become my most profitable relationships, and that's okay. For example, Henry is a plumber. He's one of my best buddies. We love fishing on the rare early afternoon out. However, Henry doesn't often come in contact with people I generally do business with. However, when he does, and I'm confident he will, he will pass me a referral."

"Let's look under my Profitability list. These members make me the most money. I am their go-to service provider for my industry. A lot of referrals I get from them don't even need to be sold. It's like free closed business."

"Kind of like you for me," I said, recognizing instantly what he was explaining.

"Exactly. When I send a referral your way, I always say, 'Ken is the best company in town to help you with what you need.' That's why they're a done deal when they give you a call. You just have to put a shiny red bow on them. That is my favorite kind of referral to give."

"There are different *kinds* of referrals?"

Jim laughed. "We've only just begun."

There was way more to networking than I'd thought. I looked forward to learning and moving into Jim's Profitability column.

PRACTICE

For Mentees and Mentors

This is one of our favorite exercises for mentees to do initially and mentors to do about once a year—just like going for an annual check-up. The trick is to be honest with yourself. Don't sugarcoat it. Take out a piece of paper and write Visibility, Credibility and Profitability across the top. Now draw lines down to the bottom, creating three columns. We're going to do this twice, so feel free to get another chart prepped.

VISIBILITY -----> CREDIBILITY -----> PROFITABILITY

Rank the members of your networking group in one of the three columns. Here's a quick reminder:

VISIBILITY means they know you and your business exist. They are aware of you. Communication is in its infancy.

CREDIBILITY means the person finds you honest, trustworthy and ready to receive their referral. They might have given you at least one referral that turned into business.

PROFITABILTY means that person is a source of recurring referrals. You are their go-to business for whatever you offer. There exists a mutually beneficial relationship.

If you're new to networking, the second VCP sheet might be more telling since the first sheet could have your entire group lumped under Visibility. Take a look at who the referral sources have been for your business. If you're a real estate agent, is there a mortgage banker who sends you referrals? If you're a chiropractor, is there a physical trainer who sends you clients? Don't list individual customers/clients. Focus on the referral sources or acquaintances who send you business.

The goal of networking is to get more contacts into the Profitability column. **Doing so is a process, not a formula.**

V + C DOES NOT EQUAL P @IVANMISNER

VISIBILITY + CREDIBILITY ≠ PROFITABILITY

IT IS A REFERRAL PROCESS, NOT A FORMULA

CHAPTER 7

THE FRIENDSHIP FACTOR

I went straight back to the office and did the same thing Jim had done. Reminding myself to be honest, I searched my brain for the sources of my referrals. To my dismay, the left side of the sheet was heavier than my right. Jim was the sole caretaker of the Profitability column. I had two contacts listed under Credibility and fourteen under Visibility. Other than Jim, I hadn't bothered to list the members of my networking group. They didn't know me yet.

Being a numbers guy, I added up rough totals of the business I'd received from each column. Jim's Profitability column outweighed the rest. What did that tell me? I needed to fill my VCP columns and earn the right to move my new networking companions up the ladder.

Being the eager student, I called Jim and told him about the results of my VCP exercise.

"Don't worry," he said. "That's pretty common if you haven't been actively networking. Most businesses are just trying to survive. Heck, when I did my first VCP analysis I didn't have one person in the Profitability column. You're way ahead of where I was when I started!"

"When can we have another session?" I asked.

"How about tomorrow? We've gotta eat lunch, right?"

"Perfect. My treat."

+++

The next day I was ready. I'd stayed up late working on orders and got home after Heidi had gone to bed. Jim's company was keeping us hopping. The excitement only increased when I imagined my own small business attaining the same level of success.

I purposefully got to the Asian bistro fifteen minutes early to make sure the waiter let me pay the bill. Jim was notorious for sneaking the tab. Not this time. I owed him too much and hoped that this would be a tiny step toward repaying his kindness.

To my dismay, Jim had already reserved a booth at the back of the restaurant. He motioned me over, and I knew he'd already tipped off the waiter. Smiling and shaking my head, I walked up to the table and sat down.

"You're here early," he noted with a sly grin.

"Yeah. I was hoping to beat you to the bill for once."

He shrugged as if to say it wasn't a big deal.

"You sounded excited over the phone. Was there something you wanted me to review?" Jim asked.

"The VCP lesson really got me thinking. How can I jump-start the process and build more trusting relationships?"

Jim chuckled. "It's actually easier than you might think. Let me tell you what I did so you don't make the same mistake. When I joined the group, I was in full-on 'GO' mode. My business was struggling, and I was extremely

45

motivated to make more money. I came on a little strong. Every meeting I hounded my new friends about how I could help them with my services. I carried business cards in both pockets and handed them out to the group like I was giving candy on Halloween. Finally, a veteran member pulled me aside and told me the secret."

At the mention of a secret, I sat up straighter and leaned in. "What was the secret?"

Jim looked around like he was making sure no one was listening, and then in a voice barely above a whisper, he said, "Make friends—build relationships."

"What?" I really thought I'd misheard.

"I said, make friends."

"That's the secret?"

Jim nodded, grinning and obviously amused at the confused look on my face. "Look, **networking isn't about putting your business card in as many hands as you can.** That was my mistake. Networking is all about making friends and building relationships within the context of helping each other in business. **When times are tough, people don't hesitate to fire a vendor; but they think twice about firing a friend.** They do their best to continue to work with you. Let me ask you a question. Would you rather do business with a friend or with a stranger?"

"A friend, of course."

"Why?"

"Because my friends are people I know and trust."

"Ding, ding, ding. You win the prize. Most of the men and women I see failing at networking are those who don't make it personal enough. The saying that we should separate business and personal is total baloney. Ask anyone whether they'd choose to do business with a friend or stranger, and I'll bet the vast majority would pick the friend."

"So why do so many experts talk about keeping business, well, business?" I asked.

"It's a matter of being professional. Doing business with your friends is still business. Remember earlier when I explained that the group has rules in part because a network's strength *and* weakness is that it's made up of friends who wouldn't otherwise hold each other accountable? It's true. Most of us are friends."

It made sense. I could name four vendors who'd been friends either in college or high school.

"What happens when one of your business friends lets you down?" I questioned.

"That's the point exactly. Being professional means delivering on your promises. You have to provide the same level of superior service to your friends as you do to your regular customers. You don't get a free pass. There won't be many friends left if you screw that up."

"Okay. How do I make more friends in this context?"

Before he could answer, the waiter came to take our orders. I was starving and asked for more than I was going to eat. Once he left, Jim continued.

"We have a simple thing called a 1-2-1. It's basically a sit-down like we're having right now. I like to schedule mine for an hour, thirty minutes for each of us."

"What do you do in a 1-2-1?"

"At first you're just getting to know each other. It's kind of like dating. Where are you from? Do you have a family? Where did you go to school? Stuff like that. It's good to start with the personal first. We are, after all, trying to make new friends. Next, it's on to business. We share what our companies do, and, more importantly, the kind of customers we're looking for," said Jim

"But I thought we already did that in the weekly meeting."

"We do, but our quick weekly presentation isn't long enough to get into the why and how. During a 1-2-1, I like to have a list of examples of my current clients, the types of clients I'm looking for and referral sources I want to meet. When we're that specific, it's a lot easier for our networking partners to give us referrals."

"Isn't that a little nitpicky?"

"Why? Because I'm telling you *exactly* who I want to do business with? No. It's important to spell it out. Your networking partners will want that. Don't let them guess. If they're looking to bring you referrals, they need to know that you want to talk to businesses with up to ten employees or families who've just moved to the area. That's a lot better than saying, 'I want anyone you know who needs my service.' It may sound counter-intuitive, but instead of asking for everything under the sun, it's better to zoom in and be laser-specific. What if they don't completely understand what you do? Then you don't get anything."

It was challenging to wrap my brain around the concept. I was so used to asking for any and all business. As I came to the realization that I'd hindered my efforts by being too vague, the waiter brought our order. My eyes widened when I saw the huge plate of food he placed in front of me.

"I hope you're hungry," laughed Jim.

I nodded and attacked the noodles as Jim continued the lesson.

"It's important to have a 1-2-1 with every member of our group as soon as you can. Start with the members who you think would be prime referral sources. You'll also want to have additional mentoring meetings with other group members as part of BNI's mentoring programs. When you have enough 1-2-1s, you'll know the personalities of the group. That's when you can really connect on a higher level of trust."

"How much time does that take?" I asked, already knowing that my daily allotment of time was limited.

Jim shrugged. "It depends. I know how busy you are. That's why it will be vitally important to have a focused approach to this. But let me remind you, focused does not mean robotic, and I'm not saying you should just go through the motions. You want to connect with your networking partners on a deeper level. Remember, you're building friendships first and business later."

"I think I can do that."

"I know you can. Now, let me tell you who I think you should start with."

PRACTICE

For Mentees and Mentors

If you're new to networking, or rekindling your fire, take a fresh look at how you're doing it. Networking is all about developing relationships—and then maintaining those relationships and friendships over the long haul. Imagine what you could do if you had a core group of great friends that brought you business on a consistent basis. But making friends through a networking group is especially powerful—because unlike friends who know you outside of your business, your business networking friends will hold you accountable in a way your best friend from high school likely won't.

Here's your next assignment: Make a list of the next ten 1-2-1s from within your networking group. Stagger them over the next two months. You might be eager to have a whole bunch of 1-2-1s right away—many each week. While that may sound like a good idea, you don't want to risk burn out. There's a lot to be done, but you eat an elephant one bite at a time. **Networking is more like a marathon than a sprint. Pace yourself.** Once you have your list of ten people, reach out to them and see when they have time to meet. Suggest at least two times and a location. Make it easy for them to say yes. If you're a mentor, suggest meeting with old friends and new members of your networking group to nurture and grow those relationships.

NETWORKING IS MORE LIKE A MARATHON THAN A SPRINT —PACE YOURSELF

Be prepared when you show up for your 1-2-1s. Have your personal and business bio along with two lists, your last ten customers and the kinds of referrals you're looking for. It may also be helpful to mention the referrals you *don't* want. Sometimes those are easier to remember. To facilitate these conversations, BNI uses the GAINS Exchange, where each person shares their Goals, Accomplishments, Interests, Networks, and Skills. Even if you're not a member of BNI, you can still use this approach.

Always keep in mind that it's not all about business. Have fun. Smile. Enjoy the time you spend on your 1-2-1s. Finding out about the other person as an individual is important. Get to know them and their family, as well as the business side of your relationship, and you'll become that much closer.

GOALS

THE ONE TO ONE PACK

ACCOMPLISHMENTS

SKILLS

NETWORKS

INTERESTS

CHAPTER 8

LEADS vs. REFERRALS

Jim talked about some of his favorite 1-2-1s and I laughed as I listened. He made it fun, and that gave me hope. I liked the idea of spending time face-to-face with my fellow networkers. It was easier for me than mingling in a crowded room.

"Okay. We've talked about the VCP Process, making friends, 1-2-1s...the next lesson won't take long. Tell me, what's the difference between a lead and a referral?" Jim asked.

"I don't really know. I kinda thought they were the same thing."

"Let me ask you another way. If you're looking for new business, would you rather I give you someone's name and tell you I heard they are looking for your services or would you prefer I introduce you, in person, over lunch?"

"In person, over lunch."

"That's the difference between a lead and a referral: relationship. A lead is simply data, nothing you can't get from the Internet. That person is a stranger. When I add the relationship component, it turns into a referral. **As business owners, we want referrals not leads.** Let me tell you about another one of my mistakes. Like I mentioned before, when I started networking, I was pretty gung-ho. Going on all cylinders, as they say. I was on a mission to impress the group. So what did I do? I walked in one Wednesday morning with a print out of all my clients along with their contact information. I'd made five copies. I ceremoniously gave them to the five lucky winners I'd chosen. Their looks said it all. They were not impressed and probably amused. I asked one of them why. You know what he told me?"

"What?"

"In a very non-condescending way, he told me that he could just as easily get a list of random people and call them. I remember saying, 'But these are my clients.' He smiled and asked me what made my client any less a stranger than a name picked off the Internet. I didn't have an answer. He was right. He explained how I could turn the list into something positive. Rather than give the group a list of numbers, it was much more effective to take the time to call my clients and personally introduce them to my networking partners."

"But don't some businesses want leads?"

"Sure, but don't you think they should be asking for warm referrals instead? Which call would you take? The one from a company you don't know or a call that you're expecting?"

"The one I'm expecting," I said, the explanation finally getting through my thick head.

"Of course! Just like it's important to network with friends, your clients and customers want to do business with people they know, or at least someone they feel comfortable using. When you give a referral, you are giving your stamp of approval to that person. You're saying that you're willing to put your reputation on the line to refer them business. That's why it's so important to network with people who you know will live up to your expectations."

"I guess I'd never thought about it that way before. It's kind of like vetting someone or doing a background check. I'm embarrassed to say that I've already had my office manager print off our client list. I was going to give it to you."

Jim laughed. "That just means great minds think alike! Don't forget that I made that mistake first!"

I laughed along with him as I thought ahead to the warm referrals I could give to my networking group.

PRACTICE

For Mentees

Remember the philosophy of Giver's Gain? It works perfectly for referrals. As a networker, you want to give the warmest referrals you can by building strong relationships. It's about getting to know, like and trust people. Then, it's about doing your part to support your network. **Don't make promises, just deliver.**

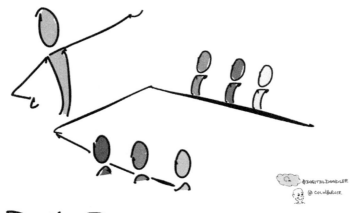

DON'T PROMISE, JUST DELIVER

Make a list of your current clients. See whom you'd feel comfortable referring to one of the members of your networking group. Make the introduction personal. Try to avoid sending a simple email. Make it red hot by initiating a conference call or going out to lunch with your referral and your networking partner. It may take extra time, but it will be time well spent. Both parties will appreciate your thoughtfulness.

For Mentors

You likely have trained your reticular activating system by now to listen for key phrases that trigger you to give a referral. Add a few new words to your reticular activating system—whatever words that someone would mention who needs the services or products of your mentee—and make an extra effort to give referrals specifically for your mentee. Doing so will likely give you a little boost in your step because you feel good about going out of your way to help a newer member of your networking group. **Remember the importance of "walking the talk." Be an example by what you do—as well as what you say.**

CHAPTER 9

PUTTING IT ALL TOGETHER

I hit a few bumps along the way, but I spent the next month doing just what Jim said: making friends. I couldn't wait for Wednesday morning and the excitement of spending time with my group of motivated salespeople.

I was getting into a routine with my 1-2-1s by taking Jim's advice and scheduling them during my lunch hour. Rather than eating behind my desk, I got to network and build relationships. It also came with the added bonus of getting me out of the office.

My employees noticed the change in attitude with comments like, "You've got so much energy" and "It's great to see you smiling." Even though we'd never talked about the hard times, they'd known it by my demeanor. I prided myself in hiding my feelings to keep the ship running straight, but I'd obviously let the façade slip. The ship was slowly getting back on course.

I liked the new me. Energy surrounded my activities. I had a purpose again. On the one hand, I loved the aspect of giving back to my networking partners, and on the other, I enjoyed the business that started to trickle in. I was on a new path and so was my company.

Jim showed me how to track the referrals I gave and the referrals I received. "It's important to know where your business comes from," he said.

It made me realize that I'd never done the same with my company. Right away I sat down with Dana and we devised a system for categorizing every new customer that came in. The afternoon exercise opened my eyes to the revenue I was already generating from my networking group. Sure, Jim was the majority of that number, but if I could develop even one more relationship to the same level, we could hire a new employee!

I showed my team how to use the system and gave them a rundown of my referral partners. Some of them they'd already met. Dana said the new system would make things a lot easier because our clients were always asking what vendor we used for this or that service. I'd unconsciously found another way to funnel referrals into my networking group.

Two months into my networking adventure, I hired a new employee. I was working too many hours, and the orders kept piling up. The move was probably long overdue, but I'd waited to hit my target monthly revenue so it wouldn't hurt our bottom line. Every week I'd reviewed incoming orders, and I found that our existing clients were also paying us more. I asked Dana why she thought that was, and she said, "It's you, Ken. We're not the only ones who've noticed the change. Our clients are happy about it, too."

The compliment humbled me. I vowed never to make the same mistake again. A company owner's attitude affects so much. I wondered how much business I'd lost because of my poor disposition.

After our next networking meeting, I cornered Jim to tell him the good news. "That is fantastic. I knew you could do it."

I was probably bouncing like a kid on a sugar high. "So what do I do next? How do I keep growing?"

Jim smiled at my excitement. "Keep doing what you're doing. Make friends. Help your referral partners. Get creative but always remember what you had to do to get here. Some people start getting more and more business like you are and they make the bonehead mistake of saying something like, **'I'm so busy, I don't have time to do this anymore.' I say to them—seriously! You get really busy and your answer is to stop doing what made you successful!!!"** Think about this before you act on that. Hire someone and keep doing what you are doing to grow. That's one of the ways to scale your business. So Ken, keep doing what you're doing and continue to hire more people. You are definitely doing the right things, and I'm really proud of your success."

"Got it. I can't imagine doing something so silly as to stop doing the things that have helped me grow my business. What's next?"

Jim said, "Tell you what. Give me a week or two to wrap up some things on my end, and then we'll talk about building a culture of referrals."

My eyes went wide. "A *culture of referrals?*"

"Yeah. For now, keep at it. I'm hearing some great things from the other members. You're connecting on a personal level and everyone you've done business with is impressed by your service. Do what I told you. Hone your skills, and then we'll move on and put the icing on the cake. Remember, networking is a marathon not a sprint. And learning is a lifelong process. You've had some great success early on, but that could all go away if you let up or fail to deliver."

"Don't worry. I won't let up. Can we go ahead and schedule that session?" I asked, eager to climb further up the mountain.

PRACTICE

For Mentees and Mentors

If you haven't done so already, create a spreadsheet to track your referrals. You might be surprised to see how enlightening of a practice this is. After you do this, make plans to strengthen your relationship with each referral partner by checking that your reticular activating system is actively listening for opportunities to give them referrals. If you're disappointed with the number of referral partners you have, that is simply more motivation to continue with your networking activities.

If you need further assistance for tracking your referrals and networking activities, write a list of actions you can take on a regular basis, and then hold yourself accountable by recording your activity. Here are some ideas to get you started:

- Attend a networking event.
- Display a referral partner's brochures in your office.
- Share a referral partner's information on social media.

- Send a thank-you card or personalized thank-you gift.
- Arrange a group activity for your referral partners.

Keeping track of your activities will help you determine what is bringing in results while doing the things you need to do to build a powerful personal network.

For a more in-depth discussion of specific networking and referral activities you can consult *Networking Like a Pro: Turning Contacts into Connections (Second Edition)* by Ivan Misner and Brian Hilliard. You can also download our free Networking Scorecard at http://IvanMisner.com/Scorecard/.

The point here is that both mentors and mentees need to be consistent and strategic in their networking and referral-generating activities.

CHAPTER 10

A CULTURE OF REFERRALS

Like numerous times before, Jim and I met over lunch. After we ordered our food at the café owned by one of our fellow BNI members, I asked Jim about his suggestions for achieving a culture of referrals. His words surprised me.

"Let's first talk about core values."

"Huh?"

"Everything stems from the core values of BNI. In the "busyness" of our day-to-day lives, it's so easy to forget what they are and why they are important. I find it's helpful for me to periodically review them, so I thought we'd discuss a few today together."

"Givers Gain is *the* principal core value of BNI. You have to be willing to give people business if you hope to get business in return. It's as simple as that. As soon as I started paying attention to the Language of Referrals and giving referrals, I noticed an uptick in the number I received. **Givers Gain is about taking off your bib and putting on an apron.**"

"What?"

"You heard me. It's about taking the bib off and putting the apron on—it's about serving more than receiving. The best networkers try to find ways to help others. They serve before they ever expect to get something in return—before they ever expect to get fed."

"Oh, wow. So, I need to take off my bib, and put on my apron. I've never thought about it like that before."

GIVERS GAIN: TAKE OFF THE BIB
                    PUT ON THE APRON

@DIGITALDOODLER
@ COLINYEARUCK

"Most people don't. But it's a helpful reminder. Here's something else to remember: **Companies that don't innovate, stagnate.**"

Jim shared yet another sound bite that I don't think I'll ever forget.

He continued, "What I mean is that traditions are important because they tell us who we are—so traditions are critical—but innovation tells us who we can become. Create a culture in your company that honors both tradition and innovation. Culture eats strategy for breakfast."

"This is great, Jim. What else do you have for me?" I was thirsty for more of his suggestions and grabbed my notebook out of my briefcase to record his advice.

"Maintain a positive attitude. **No one likes doing business or hanging out with crabby people. Most people want to do business with people who have a positive and supportive attitude.** Don't show up to a business meeting in a foul mood. Likewise, surround yourself with positive people who are on fire. **Ignorance on fire is better than knowledge on ice.** If you find people with a positive attitude who are on fire, they will make better referral partners and employees."

I was soaking up Jim's advice like a sponge and writing notes furiously.

"Recognize people who help you. Take the time to acknowledge them. Thank them. When you do, you'll find they are flattered you said a kind word and are motivated to send more business your way."

"Jim, I recall reading BNI's core values, but I guess I never thought about them in this way."

"Well, I'm not done yet," Jim quipped.

"People are much less likely to refer you if you don't have a strong relationship with them. **It's not what you know or who you know. Rather, it's how well you know each other that counts! Contrary to popular belief, networking isn't a numbers game but rather a people puzzle.**"

I felt like my hand was about to fall off from all the writing I was doing.

"Let me share with you a few more techniques that I learned from one of BNI's educational programs. Oh yeah…did I mention that lifelong learning is also a core value?"

"I know, I know…" I assured him. This idea of learning had been drilled into me already.

"You want to educate your network. Teach them the benefits of your service and help them understand the why behind what you do. You need to **empower your network to help you.**"

His words caused me to lean in, even though the general ideas behind them felt familiar at this point.

"First, you'll want to be very specific about the services and products you offer. Remember: Specific is terrific.

"Second, share the lowest common denominators of your business to your network. Break your business into easily understood parts, such as a product, service or benefit you offer to customers. **When networking, don't try to cover everything in one conversation or presentation. Strive for depth rather than breadth.**

"Third, train your sales force to look for possibilities that fit a particular mold. To do this, share with them stories of an exchange with a client that went well or tell them about an ideal business deal.

"Last, distribute marketing collateral that your network can then share when giving referrals. Put your flyers, catalogues or other materials to good use!"

I couldn't believe how much information Jim shared with me in such a short time. We only had our salads brought to us; our main meals were still back in the kitchen being prepared. To this point, I had thought I already learned quite a bit—which I had. But now the idea of lifelong learning was really sinking in.

PRACTICE

For Mentees and Mentors

It's helpful to have the core principles of BNI handy. Refer to them to keep your networking efforts on track, and use them for inspiration if you still need to determine the core values of your own business. These core values are powerful whether you are in BNI or not. **Success is the uncommon application of common knowledge.**

1. **Givers Gain:** You have to be willing to give people business if you hope to get business in return. Givers Gain is a standard that you apply to yourself and to your dealings with other people. It is the guiding principle or philosophy for BNI.

2. **Building Relationships: Networking is more about farming than it is about hunting.** It's all about

building strong professional relationships within a structured environment.

3. **Lifelong Learning:** Ongoing education is important in any field. However, networking isn't taught in colleges and universities as a stand-alone course anywhere in the world. But BNI teaches it. If you are willing, BNI has the content. You will constantly be learning how you can build a powerful, personal and professional network.

4. **Traditions + Innovation:** This sounds like a paradox. How can you focus on both? Traditions tell us who we are today as an organization. Innovation tells us who we can become as an organization. Both are valued in BNI.

5. **Positive Attitude:** Most people want to do business with people who have a positive and supportive attitude. It is important to apply this core value throughout every area of the organization.

6. **Accountability:** Success in business requires accountability...even among friends. BNI's best chapters never overlook this principle.

7. **Recognition:** From day one, recognition has been an important element and a critical organizational value. Effective recognition is so important in BNI.

CHAPTER 11

WHAT GOES AROUND COMES AROUND

Two years later...

As I hung up the phone from a call with Jim to discuss the course we have been taking through *BNI University*, I couldn't help but chuckle as I thought about that fateful day two years ago when Jim asked me to be his guest at BNI. What a change. I was in such bad shape back then. I was desperate—and didn't even realize that **desperation isn't referable**. People can smell it a mile away. I'm in such a better place now and am grateful to have Jim as my friend, mentor and client.

Just as I was wishing I could help someone like Jim has helped me, I looked out the window and noticed Denise getting out of her car, double checking that her clothes hadn't gotten wrinkled from the car ride. A new client of mine, she looked nervous.

A few minutes later, Dana walked her into the conference room to meet with me, handing her a cold bottle of water.

"Hi, Denise, it's good to see you."

"Hi, Ken," Denise stammered, as she spilled a few drops of water while opening the bottle. "There's something I'd like to talk to you about."

I knew where this was going. Bad news travels fast. I had just heard from Jim that Denise had to lay off two people at her company. And she had an outstanding invoice with me.

"Ken..." Denise struggled to get out any more words as she looked down at the table. "Look, things have been tough lately, and I lost the single most profitable account I had. I can't believe I let myself have almost all my eggs in one basket. My business is upended, and I don't know what to do. I'm wondering if we can set up a payment plan for me to make things right with your company. I'm really sorry..."

"Thank you for being upfront with me. Yes, we can work out a plan. But can I also throw you a life preserver?"

"What do you mean?"

"What if I told you that I was in your situation a couple of years ago, and I know how you can learn to turn around your business?"

"Are you serious? *You* were like *me*?"

This had a familiar ring to it and I laughed, remembering my conversation with Jim two years ago.

"I'd like to invite you to a local networking group I'm a part of. We're interviewing people in your profession to find someone who we could give all of our referrals to. I think you might make a great candidate. Why don't you come as my guest so I could introduce you to some of my best local contacts?"

"Gee, thanks, but I don't know if I have time for networking since I have to focus on sales..."

"I know what you're thinking. It wasn't my thing either. But what if I told you that over seventy percent of my company's revenue came from the people in this one networking group? *My first year of being part of the networking group was good, but the second year was amazing, and it keeps getting better.*" I then thought of my old client, Barry and said, "My network is so strong now that I have even been able to fire a problem client that I really didn't like working with!"

Denise's eyes grew wide; she leaned in to hear more and then listened intently as I began to share my story…

Thanks for reading. We hope you enjoyed the story. **If you did, please leave an online review.** Your reviews fuel this story's success.

For more information on books from Ivan Misner, go to www.IvanMisner.com.

For more information on other books by C. G. Cooper visit http://TheMentorCode.com.

MORE NETWORKING RESOURCES

BNI®: With a quarter of a million members globally, BNI is the largest business networking organization in the world. Each year, BNI generates millions of referrals, resulting in billions of dollars worth of business for its members. For general information on the organization visit **www.BNI.com**. To have someone contact you about more information, go to **http://ivan.bni.com** and complete the information request.

Networking App: If you would like to track your networking activities, check out the free Networking Scorecard app at **http://IvanMisner.com/Scorecard/**.